New Leaf

Ideas for Writing, Inspired by Trees

M.S.D. Samston

Illustrated by

Ilan Shamir

Cottonwood Press, Inc.
107 Cameron Drive
Fort Collins, CO 80525
800-864-4297
www.cottonwoodpress.com

ISBN 1-877673-52-8

Table of Contents

Trees as Inspiration for Creativity

Throughout history, the tree has played an important role in art of all kinds, from mythology and music to painting, literature, and poetry. Just a few examples:

- The tree in the Bible's Garden of Eden, the Yggdrasil tree of Norse mythology, the Bo tree of Buddhism.
- The New England woods of Nathaniel Hawthorne's *Young Goodman Brown*, Henry David Thoreau's woods in *Walden*, the tree in Sarah Orne Jewett's "A White Heron," the forbidden forest in the Harry Potter series, the tree that Scout and Jem use to communicate with Boo Radley in *To Kill a Mockingbird*.
- Peter Paul and Mary's song "Lemon Tree," the 1940s song "Don't Sit Under the Apple Tree," the enduring popularity of "Tie a Yellow Ribbon 'Round the Ole Oak Tree," Billy Holiday's song "Strange Fruit."
- The cypress trees and olive trees painted by Vincent Van Gogh, Gustav Klimt's birch trees, Claude Monet's poplar trees, the oak trees photographed by Ansel Adams.

- Joyce Kilmer's "Trees" and Robert Frost's "Stopping By Woods on a Snowy Evening."
- The medieval forest of Arthurian legend, the woods that lure Hansel and Gretel, Robin Hood's Sherwood Forest, the enchantment of the woods in Shakespeare's *Midsummer Night's Dream*.

The list could go on and on.

What is it about the tree that inspires creativity?

Perhaps the strength, the seeming permanence of the tree — at least when compared with the short life span of humans — inspires artists to attempt creations of equal permanence.

Perhaps the life cycle of the tree encourages different perspectives. With its changing appearance in winter, spring, summer and fall, the average tree by its very nature may inspire a person to look at the world in different ways.

Perhaps the beauty of the tree, in all its forms, makes men and women want to create beauty of their own. What is more beautiful, for example, than a cottonwood tree in winter, the branches outlined against a pink and gold sunset? Or the fluttering lime green of aspen leaves against white bark? Or a cherry tree in full bloom?

Perhaps the sheer variety of trees inspires us. From towering redwoods to tiny bonsai, from dark pines to bright birches, from spare palms to dense hemlocks and resplendent oaks, trees come in so many shapes, sizes and forms. Perhaps that variety inspires us to emulate nature's creativity.

Perhaps the mystery of the tree sparks our imaginations. What lurks in the leaves of a tall oak, or in the dense growth of a rainforest? What shapes can we imagine in the branches reaching toward the sky, or in the patterns of the bark? Where do the roots stretch and how far, how deep?

Perhaps the tree simply tickles all of our senses. We hear the sound of leaves rustling in the breeze, the moan of pine boughs in the dead of winter, the soft plunk of ripe fruit falling to the ground. We marvel at the sight of a fiery red maple in fall, or the perfect majesty in a row of palm trees. We feel the cool slickness of a glossy cottonwood leaf and the prickliness of a pinecone. We taste the sweetness of a fresh-picked peach in springtime or the tartness of a crisp apple in fall. We breathe the sweet fragrance of magnolia blossoms or the rich scent of pine.

Whatever the reasons may be, the tree somehow taps the imagination.

Just as the tree has inspired the writing prompts in *A New Leaf*, allow the prompts to help you tap your own imagination. As you write, remember that you are following a long and rich tradition.

Writing Prompts

Describing

A cottonwood leaf drifts,

reluctantly,

to the earth

and rests.

*L*ook, really LOOK at a leaf from a tree.
Describe its shape, its edges, its veins,
its color, its texture, its size.
Capture the leaf, in words.

*D*escribe a tree memory.

Do you remember leaf-crunching walks with a friend?

Daydreaming at the base of a poplar tree?

Falling from a branch? Swinging on a tire swing?

Seeking shelter in a sudden rain?

Remember the details.

How did you feel? What did you see?

What did you smell? Taste? Hear?

Be as specific as possible.

Describe a kind of tree that lives
in your part of the country.
What kind of a tree is it?
A cottonwood? An aspen? A palm?
A birch? A redwood? A maple? A weeping willow?
Where do you see it?
In yards, in parks, along the highway?
In forests, on the plains, along rivers?
Describe the tree so that someone who has never seen
that kind of tree might picture it.

Describe a view from under a tree, looking up.

Describe a view from under a tree,
looking down.

Describe a view from the top of a tree,

as you imagine it.

Describe a tree in your past or present
that holds some kind of meaning for you,
for whatever reason.
Perhaps it was a tree outside the window
of your childhood home,
or a tree that your little brother climbed.
Perhaps it is a tree you helped a child plant,
or a tree you sit under at the park.
What attracts you to the tree?
Describe its meaning to you.

*H*ave you ever had a tree house?
If so, describe it. What did you like about it?
How did you spend your time there?
Remember every detail.

If you never had a tree house,
or even if you did,
imagine your ideal tree house.
Describe it.
What would it look like?
How would it feel to be in it?
How would you spend your time there?

*D*escribe a tree

in winter . . .

in spring . . .

in summer . . .

in fall . . .

Observe the activity that takes place on or around a tree you "know."
Perhaps it is the tree you see every day when you walk your dog,
or a tree in your backyard,
or a tree in a pot on a terrace of an apartment building.
Do birds land on the branches?
Does a dog nap under it?
Do children climb it?
Describe the action that takes place near the tree.

*P*eople often say, "Money doesn't grow on trees."

But wouldn't it be nice if it did?

Suppose you could pick money off a tree, like cherries.

Describe what you would do with that money.

Trees give us many gifts.

Describe some of the gifts that trees give to our world.

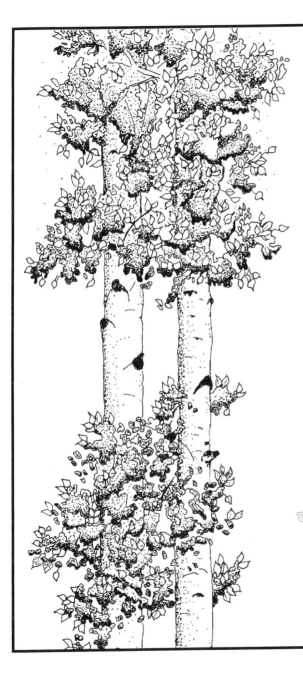

Imagining

Like a leaf

drifting on a breeze,

the imagination drifts

to unexpected destinations.

A leaf drifts off on a breeze, and you follow.

Imagine where you will go,

what you will do.

Describe your journey.

*I*magine a world without trees.
(Ignore the fact that without trees
there wouldn't be enough oxygen to support life!)
What would the earth be like?
How would the world be different?

*I*magine that you could create a new tree
and grow whatever you wanted on it,
other than money.
What type of tree would you create?
Where would it grow?
Describe your tree.

Imagine the world from a tree's perspective.
Describe how the tree might view its surroundings.

Trees are used in the production of paper.

Imagine a world without paper.

What would a paperless society be like?

How would our world be different?

Explain.

*I*magine all the generations represented in your family tree.

If you could visit any one person from your family's past,

who would you choose?

Why?

What questions would you ask your relative?

How do you imagine the conversation might go?

37

$\mathcal{C}$hoose a tree you see often.

What if it were a person?

Imagine what kind of person it would be.

Describe its personality.

*W*hat if your family or friends were trees instead of people?

Imagine what kind of tree each would be.

Explain.

*W*hat if you were a tree instead of a person?
Imagine what kind of tree you would be.

Explain.

Reflecting

A budding leaf

holds

the promise of spring

and

infinite possibilities.

Think about the way a leaf drifts on the air,
aimless, yet graceful.
When have you been aimless, yet graceful?

$\mathcal{W}$hat does it mean to "remember your roots"?
Explain.

If you look at a cross section of a tree trunk,
the rings help indicate the age of the tree.
These rings are called growth rings.
In terms of milestones in your life,
write about your own growth rings.
What are the most significant events of your lifetime?
How have they helped you grow?

*Have you ever been lost
in a forest, the woods, or a jungle?
Were you afraid? What were you afraid of?
Write about the experience.*

*W*hat are you afraid of now in your life?

Why?

Explain.

What does it mean "to go out on a limb"?

What do you feel strongly about?

Would you go out on a limb for it?

Explain.

Many trees produce nuts
that grow inside a hard, protective shell.
Do you have a "shell"?
How strong is it?
What does it take to break it?

The central root of a tree is called the taproot.
Besides providing the tree with nourishment,
this taproot is the tree's main "anchor."
What is your main anchor?
What gives you stability and a sense of "rootedness"?

In the fall, trees shed their leaves.
In the spring, they bud with new leaves.
The cycle of change and renewal
happens over and over again every year.
Write about a time in your life when
you experienced a similar cycle.
What "leaves" did you shed?
What leaves did you grow?

The branches of trees often need to be trimmed
so they can grow taller.
What in your life would you like to trim?
How would this trimming
make your life better?
How would it help you grow?

*W*hat can we learn from trees?

Explain.

Responding

Leaves rustle,

like our thoughts,

with the

slightest encouragement.

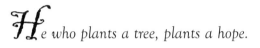

He who plants a tree, plants a hope.

— Lucy Larcom, *Plant a Tree*

How can a tree represent hope?

Explain.

*A society grows great when old men plant trees
whose shade they know they shall never sit in.*

— Greek proverb

What does this quotation mean to you?
Explain.

Of all man's works of art, a cathedral is greatest.
A vast and majestic tree is greater than that.

— Henry Ward Beecher

Do you agree?
Why or why not?

$\mathcal{S}$olitary trees, if they grow at all, grow strong.

— Sir Winston Churchill

What do you think is Churchill's meaning?

Explain.

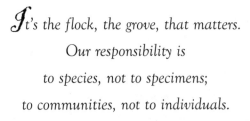

It's the flock, the grove, that matters.
Our responsibility is
to species, not to specimens;
to communities, not to individuals.

— Sara Stein, *Noah's Garden*

Is it true that our responsibility should be to the grove,
rather than to the individual?
Why or why not?

*The tree which moves some to tears of joy is in the eyes of others
only a green thing that stands in the way.*

— William Blake, *The Letters*

What do you think Blake means?
Explain.

The apple never falls too far from the tree.

— A proverb

This old saying is about more than apples.
What do you think it means?

Do not be afraid to go out on a limb . . .
That's where the fruit is.

— Anonymous

Do you agree?
Why or why not?

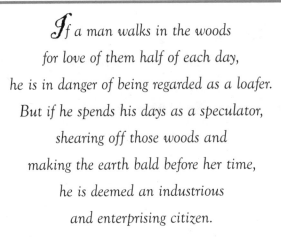

If a man walks in the woods
for love of them half of each day,
he is in danger of being regarded as a loafer.
But if he spends his days as a speculator,
shearing off those woods and
making the earth bald before her time,
he is deemed an industrious
and enterprising citizen.

— Henry David Thoreau

Thoreau is making a comment on society.
What does he mean?

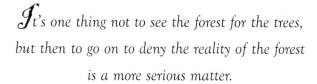

It's one thing not to see the forest for the trees,
but then to go on to deny the reality of the forest
is a more serious matter.

— Paul Weiss

What could Weiss mean?
Can you think of situations where his comment might apply?
Explain.

I am myself and what is around me,

and if I do not save it, it shall not save me.

— Jose Ortega y Gasset

How does this quotation relate to trees?

Investigating

Turn over a new leaf.

You never know what

you might discover.

*F*ind information about an unusual tree.
What makes it unusual?
Some trees you might consider:

tuliptree

sassafrass

banyan tree

Joshua tree

huon pine

talipot palm

monkey puzzle tree

dragon tree

Wollemi pine

*F*ind out more about one of these famous trees:

Fairmont Park Chinese Scholar

Lone Cyprus

Treaty Oak

Mendota Mdewakanton Dakota Ceremonial Oak

Scythe Tree

Chatham House Catalpa

Emancipation Oak

Luna Tree

Dueling Oaks

Evangeline Oak

Wye Oak

Major Oak of Sherwood Forest

The Shambles Oak

Middleton Oak

Torture Tree

Bodhi Tree

The Chestnut Tree of a Hundred Horses

Cypress of Thule

What makes the tree you have chosen famous?
Explain

*W*ho was Johnny Appleseed?

Find out more about him.

Summarize your findings.

*W*ho was John Muir?

Find out about his connection to trees.

Explain.

*W*hat happened to the American chestnut tree,
which used to stand so majestically
all over a large area of North America?
Explain.

*R*ecently, the National Arbor Day Foundation held
a nationwide election to choose America's national tree.
Over 100,000 people helped to vote the oak tree as our national tree.
The five trees receiving the most votes were
the oak, the redwood, the dogwood, the maple and the pine.
What would you nominate as our national tree?

Why?

*W*hat is a rainforest?

Where are rainforests located?

Why is the destruction of the rainforest a serious matter?

Explain.

*F*ind out how trees helped farmers during the Great Depression. Explain.

Trees helped the United States battle the Great Depression as part of Franklin Roosevelt's Soil Conservation Service. Explain how.

In mythology, a willow tree was sacred to Osiris.

Who was Osiris?

Why was the tree considered sacred?

Explain.

*W*hat other trees have been held sacred in various religions and myths?
Choose one and tell its story.

*W*hat is a controlled burn?

What is clear cutting?

Find out about each as a method

of keeping naturally set fires from burning out of control.

What are the advantages and disadvantages of controlled burns?

What are the advantages and disadvantages of clear cutting?

Explain.

*M*any people worry that too much logging is destroying our wooded lands.
Many others believe that logging is an important industry that provides jobs.
Find out more about the pros and cons of logging.
What do you think about this complicated issue?
Explain.

Some scientists believe that genetically-modified trees
will help to preserve the environment by producing trees
that grow more wood, more quickly, on less acreage.
Opponents worry that genetically-modified trees will cross-pollinate
with existing trees and eventually destroy trees as we know them.
Learn more about both sides of the issue.
What is your opinion?
Explain.

Creating

A sparkle of sunshine

playing on leaves

creates

pictures in the mind . . .

and

infinite possibilities.

*Trees have inspired many similes and metaphors
that describe human behavior. Just a few of them:*

shaking like a leaf

tall as a tree

skinny as a twig

thighs like tree trunks

barking up the wrong tree

turning over a new leaf

like a babe in the woods

Create some new similes and metaphors, using trees as your inspiration.

Consider all the parts of a tree:

*roots, leaves, pine cones, needles,
branches, boughs, fruit, acorns, twigs, etc.*

Imagine a radio program called "MysTREE Theater."
The last line of one radio play is this:
"They all stood in the shade of that cottonwood tree, staring.
They knew it was over."
Write the radio play.

*W*rite an alphabet book on the subject of trees.

A is for . . ,

B is for . . . ,

C is for . . . ,

etc.

In Greek mythology, a tree figures prominently in the story
of the naming of the city of Athens.
The goddess Athena and the god Poseidon are in competition
for having the leading city in Greece named after them.
Each is to provide a gift to the city, and
the citizens will choose what they feel is the more valuable gift.
Poseidon offers the city a spring that flows with salt water.
Athena offers the city a simple and plain olive tree.
The citizens decide that Athena's gift is better
because the tree offers them life, food, and economy.
Thus, they name the city "Athens," after Athena.
Create your own myth involving a tree.

Forests can be thick and dark and scary places.
Some believe fairy tales were first written
to frighten young children so they would not
wander into the woods and get hurt.
Write a fairy tale that features a forest
and that teaches a child a moral or lesson.

Below is the first line of a story. Finish the story.

The wedding took place where they had first met — under a palm tree . . .

Below is the first line of a story. Finish the story.

No one knew what was buried under the tree, but everyone was afraid to find out . . .

Below is the first line of a story. Finish the story.

The child huddled under the tree . . .

*W*rite a poem, comparing something or someone to a tree.

Ideas:

How is life like a tree?

How is your grandfather like a tree?

How is your personality like a tree?

How is love – or some other emotion – like a tree?

*J*oyce Kilmer's famous poem begins,
"I think that I shall never see,
a poem lovely as a tree."
Create an eight-line poem,
with all lines rhyming with "tree."

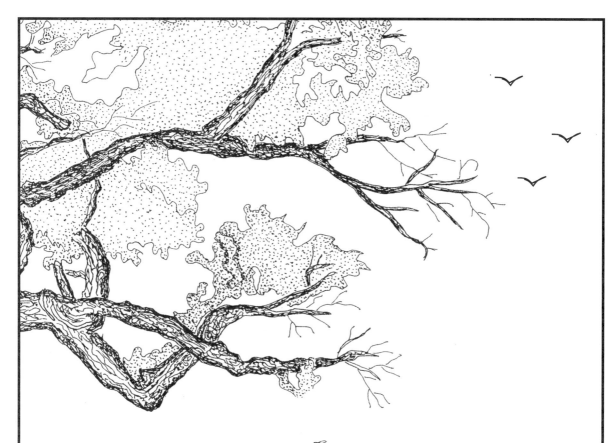

Keep a green tree in your heart

and perhaps a singing bird will come.

— Chinese proverb

Author. M.S.D. Samston is a pseudonym for the staff writers at Cottonwood Press: Mary Gutting, Sarah Stimely, Stacy Hosek, Dawn DiPrince, Samantha Prust, and Cheryl Miller Thurston.

Illustrator. Ilan Shamir, whose name means "protector of trees" celebrates the beauty of nature through art, storytelling, authoring books and performing. A simple gift of kindness received on his sixth birthday, a magnolia tree, has sparked a lifetime of appreciation and celebration of nature. Trees have touched in him a passion for growth of the soul and the wildness of life.

Shamir is the president of Your True Nature, Inc., in Fort Collins, Colorado. He offers performance keynotes and educational programs and is the author of Advice from a Tree® books and journals. Website: http://www.yourtruenature.com.

With *A New Leaf*, Cottonwood Press, Inc., is participating in the 100% Replanted program. This innovative program plants trees to replace paper and wood products used by companies and individuals. To find out more about how to participate, visit http://www.replanttrees.org.

To order more copies of A New Leaf . . .

Please send me _____ copies of *A New Leaf*. I am enclosing $9.95, plus shipping and handling ($3.50 for one book, $2.00 for each additional book). Colorado residents add 30¢ sales tax per book. Total amount $_____.

Name _____

(School) _____
(Include only if using school address.)

Address _____

City _____ State _____ Zip Code _____

Method of Payment:

❑ Payment enclosed   ❑ Credit Card   ❑ Purchase Order (must include)

Credit Card# _____Expiration Date _____

Signature _____

Send to: COTTONWOOD PRESS INC.
107 Cameron Drive
Fort Collins, CO 80525

1·800·864·4297
www.cottonwoodpress.com